The Upward Curve of Earth and Heavens

The Upward Curve
of
Earth and Heavens

by

Lester Graves Lennon

STORY LINE PRESS

ASHLAND, OREGON

Published by Story Line Press, Three Oaks Farm, PO Box 1240, Ashland, OR 97520-0055

This publication was made possible thanks in part to the generous support of the National Endowment for the Arts, the Nicholas Roerich Museum, the Andrew W. Mellon Foundation, and our individual contributors.

Book design by Lysa McDowell

Library of Congress Cataloging-in-Publication Data

Lennon, Lester Graves, 1947–
        The upward curve of earth and heavens/by Lester Graves Lennon.
            p. cm.
        ISBN 1-58654-014-9
        I. Title.

        PS3612.E364 U69 2002
        811'.6—dc21   2001049801

NATIONAL
ENDOWMENT
FOR THE ARTS

For

Deborah Meg

my dear wife who enhances the world with her beauty

&

Megan Elizabeth

our extraordinarily resourceful and radiant daughter

TABLE OF CONTENTS

Section I   Finding Beauty Lost

Section II   The Upward Curve of Earth and Heavens

Section III   Shorter Poems on Women

Section IV   Longer Poems

Section V Closing Poems

Section I

Finding Beauty Lost

Part 1: Ingredients

(In memory of Rita Levine)

This is an Israeli bus, public transport
for mountain towns on narrow cliff-side roads.

Here is a man, his home is Palestine,
his papers stamped in order, his purpose raw.

Somewhere his dearest friend must sit or lie,
never to rise from occupation's blows.

There rides a lawyer, drained by law and men,
renewed with promise in her Promised Land.

Now the man stands, lurches to driver's wheel,
screams his friend's tallest name over the cliff.

Here blinks the pilgrim, sentenced to life's wheelchair,
jerking to death within her sister's arms.

Part 2: Master of Men

I break men's bones. I wreck their hardened will.
Unseen I plot their capture. Too late they see.
They curse. I break them. Mercy fills their eyes.
I break them. When they scream for God, I show
them God's rough altar stained.

I open covered beauty to discover
when best to skewer, which fork will tighten pain.
I watch the river's splendor grow as hope
flows out on mucus, tears and blood's fear stream.
En prise, it's washed away.

Our nation once could pray with doors unlocked,
amazed. Now gates click shut. Men stoop through mazes.
Our duty is to clear our land of scheming
pawns, secret queens, who soil responsibility.
We show them cleaner lines.

To pier the brain of Satan, I would hammer
nails through the bishops' mouths to heaven's roof.
The gloved fist raised in purpose must hold faith
to fall where Abraham's obedient knife,
unchecked, would fall in mate.

(Note: "En prise" is a chess term used to describe a completely
unprotected piece.)

Part 3: John the Revelator

The genius call may soar on jazz-laid tracks,
its beauty vigorous, new: Louis Armstrong's
young '20's strut with horn from fat New Orleans;
fey Lester Young's cool presidential swing,
mid '30's, Kansas City; Charlie 'Bird'
Parker's impassioned, plosive life-gorged flights,
late '40's, the 'Big Apple'; Coltrane hears
Monk's calling, "Coltrane! Coltrane! (damn Prestige!),"
New York, late '50's, Riverside recording.

His ballads were the most exquisite played.
Atlantic lovers hushed with love would ride
his impulse into lush life not enough.
Like husbands flush with song-drenched homes who ask,
"Is this all?" he could not hear discord's sharpening
fall rise in questions pushed as perfection's quest.

"Remember, Trane, perfection's purest notes
ring silent chords. The less you play, the more
we'll hear you say. New music's just new once.
Your music's new each time the heart connects.
The straightest line thru art to ear ain't straight,
strikes sure. Ain't perfect but it's pure," said Monk.

"Perfection's purest notes, Monk, roar from chaos."

As John, the music's bannered Revelator,
his psalms, in torrents, raised ascension's shout,
pursuing Love's supreme deliverance.
He blew to reach the river's other side
and lost the side of beauty he'd unfurled.
His heart would hurl the engineer's alarm,
its screeching prayer careening, hurtling towards
the jagged break in bridge tracks cliff-air climbing.

Part 4: Team Player

Bill Robinzine? Oh, man why you ask me?
That boy was just one crazy motherfucka.
You never knew what he was gonna do.
Like the time Chocolate Thunder slammed the ball
over poor Bill so hard the backboard cracked
like a rifle shot, the glass explodin, rainin,
just pouring down, the players frozen shocked.
Then BAM get outta here, save your ass, NOW.
There's Bill, you've seen the tape, he's hoppin, dancin,
runnin, arms over head and ears like he's
heard somethin terrible; and tears, boy's sobbin.
Never seen nothin like it on the court.
Don't get me wrong, you wanted Robinzine
on your team; big-toothed barrel-chested horse
would work the boards, set picks, nice short-range jumper.
Team man, that's key; he loved the team, felt needed.

But his knee, always the knee.
Folks were just gettin bigger like the money:
fresh corn-fed farm boys, fear-fed ghetto kids.
And Bill sure wasn't no Ice, no Silk; he had
to shove and bang the boys hard to survive.
Sad thing his leaving. Basketball was all.
You knew it would be rough alone. Those strange
doe eyes were way too big to hide his tender
insides. But this, so damn quick, suicide?
It made me think real fast of Chocolate's dunk
and Bill's protectin his head, movin wild
like he just knows he hears that future shot,
and misses what he's runnin from so crazy
he's runnin to so hard.

Part 5: Robert's Compasses

Robert, in black leather bare-cheeked chaps,
black DASI sprouting from moon white ass,
sporting your "Nigger" white-on-black badge
you hunt your next bent-buck of the night.

Climber, feasting on high gallery
rungs, circling your models' circean
circles, the gaunt disquiet mounts, dis-
membering your night-framed Circinus.

Feeder, spreading your vengeance-feed as
orchids composed for gravestone orchards,
tonight's flower is yesterday's whip
wilting in the squandered light, glaring.

(Note: Circinus is a small galaxy in the southern hemisphere
shaped like a pair of drawing compasses.)

Part 6: Confession

> "Painting is poetry seen not heard; and poetry,"
> I'm quoting here, "is painting heard not seen."
> —Leonardo Da Vinci

I will tell you what I heard in three paintings.

A print of Dieric Bouts', "The Martyrdom
of Saint Erasmus," hung
above my bed before my ordination.
Erasmus shone as my Saint Elmo lacking
the fire, emblazoned, dazzling over mast,
blazing in me (sea storm, unnamed, electric).

I wanted grace like his, blank, limpid languorous,
genteelly tied to torturer's low table.
His stomach wound's near bloodless, narrow feminine
lips open to the sailors' apparatus:
the winching windlass wrapping his intestines
round and round; his life unstrung like twine.

Legend says lightning struck his martyr ground,
left none harmed, gave all wonder.
And ever after sailors stormed at sea
called him their patron, formed him with windlass arm.
My Patron too until, amazed, "The Blinding
of Samson," Rembrandt's dark view, gripped my gaze.

Stark grime and grit frame grimace, stained teeth grind;
stern steeled men grimly strain, planting their stake
deeper in clenched eye's hole as his blood blooms.
The still great force ravaged by greater force.
In ruptured eye I saw my anus bud
ravished, released to rapture's storming flower.

It was my church's charge to minister
men's souls in celibacy that denied
my sweltering sea's canto naming names,
inflaming flesh my healing charge should ease.
I challenged God to show me music greater
than music men, untamed, flamed in my body.

In wounded places I found passion's greatest
need hidden in heart-hardened fugitive
disguises: outlaw biker, brawling sailor,
more lord than Lord Apollo.
Each one's rapt mystery, intimate, glorious,
unwrapping acts abhorred, condemned as sin.

The corposant in neon blues and reds
signaled from street signs, flashed from flesh in thunder,
warnings ignored as swelling numbers numbed.
Some nights to pump up heat I wore my collar.
Most thought it drag, all grew harder when feeling
the church-marked son kneeling in holes of glory.

Eyes blackened, bloodied; body bare, found bound,
X'd like Saint Andrew, saltire on the bed.
Martyr-manqué, priest-errant, erring deeply,
I lay there not a Rembrandt but a Titian,
his satyr, Marsyas. I was becoming
my final print: "The Death of Marsyas."

The satyr challenged bright Apollo's musical
prowess and lost. The painting shows his judgment:
composed, he hangs by his hoofs upside down;
knives peel his skin; he will be flayed alive,
half human half my hidden other thing
my faith assails but says it loves my soul.

Each man who took me, each minute taken there,
became strained notes where once sheer splendor soared.
Against flesh song, against religion's cant,

within my vows, I heard the call of God
again; and knew I must confess, give penance,
repent with my profound act of contrition.

To eviscerate my sin,
I bent for stakes' bare penetration, finding
the liquid lightning's executioner
seed in me, seeding blindness, flowering AIDS.
Its braille blooms blossom, twisting threads from canvas,
my life unwound line by line, pound by pound.

I spent my youth a hagiolater,
this life will bear no hagiography
on broken vows, slow suicide, the wasting.
My church can't love my homosexuality
but has embraced me as repentant victim
in burning need of solace and forgiveness.

Section II

The Upward Curve
of Earth and Heavens

Things I Have Seen

I have been called. Now, I must answer.
I have seen things, seen them with my heart;
been there, been part, been violator
and violated, been admiral
and his sailor. I must bear witness,
leave safe harbor offered by silence,
unfurl my fear before scrawling death
and chart my passage through our great sprawl;
for I, as you, connect to all things.

I Love You. You Are So Beautiful

"I love you," he whispered, caressing
my cock, growing hard, drugs kicking in.
"You are so beautiful," he said, hand
on my head, my black descent to his
blonde crotch. Who is this dude: kinda bland,
strange sweet eyes, real taste for darker brands?
I've seen him with younger bloods and Dwight.
Haven't seen 'em. Not hard. Where's the light?

"I love you," I whispered, your hand on
my root (its dark life, engorged), the drops
taking hold. "You are so beautiful."
My hand on your head, your last lovely
descent. Our life's so hard, the future
vacant. I want to save your beauty,
shield you from things I've seen, the awful
thing I've now become. You're nice, you call
me 'Jeffrey,' not 'Jeff.' I won't forget
you. I'll keep your tongue, taste it again.
"I love you. You are so beautiful."

The Darkness Beyond

"Well, brother, see you in the darkness
beyond." Strong glass between us, the cold
murder still hot in his eyes. His life
his last execution. His nation
keeling, heeled to blind-eyed killing of
killers who kill expecting to be
killed. We call for death's awkward descents
(their mock sails of justice mocking us)
to efface bad seed sown, sadly, grown
to strangle life's ascents; as if poor
soil poorly tilled should yield only crops
inured to history's back acres.
We plough with our engaging reapers
away from healers to enraged ground.

Like him, I've heard the knife speak its clicked
tongue of slash and puncture, a morose
morse code of honor in death—hot eye
to dying eye—when disrespects fly,
warnings go unheeded and settlings
rise in handle gently pulsing; its
blade tightly locked in heart's shattered light.
God help us killing is too easy,
revenge too loose, forgiveness too tight.

Call and Woo

I have known the killer's call and woo,
his snarl sheathed softly beneath the smile.
I have been there kneeling between his
legs, knowing death comes when he comes; death,
hard in my mouth, leaking its terror,
squirming to expose me. How stupid,
trapped by dance-floor heat, already wet,
sweat beaming: "Watch me, fuck me!" Easy
to read: short short skirt, bare legs and pumps,
sleek flesh pumping like rhythmic neon.
Speed-reader offered his hand with smile,
seemed docile, a little slow. We danced
one song, part of two; he swayed, I pranced
waiting his move, the loud shameless guile
always whispered as weather report:
"Hot in here. Want to go outside?" Cock
hunger unleashed. My hand in his, my
radar down thinking the dull eyes dumb
not folding knives a click away from
horror's tongue licking my body to
dark litter on back highways. Now, left
kneeling in the unread disguise. He,
still calling me 'woman,' wants to touch
me 'there.' Me, claiming the monthly rag
(his voice so soft to contain his rage).
I have come to the line I only
imagined but thrillingly hunted,
disembarked from back bar booths and club
corners to parked cars or rented rooms.
With one misstep (a challenge offered,
fear sparked) I can ignite his evil,
I can watch me killed. I want to live
not thrill on his steel, called to his will.
Keep it up! When he's limp he'll attack
this freak who's drained his pearls, left him weak.
Don't scream! Get out of the car! Don't scream.
Gag, cough, start to talk, "Such a thick peak."
Stay alive Miss Thing. Watch for the gleam.

Haunting Hunger

Ah, Ted, wearing your hated Red Hat,
back from the dead your eyes still heat-d.

"Life I locked in the lost letter file
stamped, 'DAMAGED IN DELIVERY—NO
PENANCE DUE." I wrecked them enough. Howled
directly in their disgraced faces;
their fear, overwhelming, my power
complete. I have snared women who would
do everything not to die; abet
the soiling of their most personal
chambers. On command they would stretch their
cunt, spread their anus, beg me ('Please, please,
bite me, beat me, just don't kill me! Please
God! Mama! Da!'). Too late. Dominion
is mine, the fantasy on reel, their
future steeled in constellations like
wrists handcuffed. Tears streaming, my grandeur
ascending; natural deceivers
disarmed by the great charmer, fabled
hunter, storied prowler, preening, his
glory revealed, the trophy kneeling
before the grand inquisitor as
supreme game master who states no rules,
permits no answers, decrees only
high pain at end game each must play (I,
erect for hours): Do-as-I-say-stay-
alive. They always die. The reel must
stop. The beast roar. The hammer soar. When
they scream I cannot hear the skull crunch.
I see the shards, the mouths in silence;
their final rictus, shining, the teeth
like stars in my dark astronomy.

"Dear mother, how can you think I do
not hate you? Look how I killed them! Look

how I let you live to see this death
that grew from your womb disguised as son."

* * *

I see you so clearly, your haunting
hunger hunting the perfect kill, the
perfect power perfected in pain.
You are our best monster: beautiful,
magnetic, unknowable, alone.
In capture, resplendent in court, your
singular butchery dazzled like
new-found myth luring young women who
gathered each day, the safe-death courters,
unknowing mirrors of your unearthed
broken ones, fawns, bludgeoned by sharp light.

I see so many wounded creatures
needing to be angeled. Were there no
angels over desecrated ground
where beasts were feasting on darkened lights?
Were there no protectors alarming
with wind; no frowning sunlight's dancing
whispers: "Stop! Don't go! Look! Don't trust him!"?
Each harbors the deep witness who all
things harbors, who sounds all depths with dream-
perfect weight, routes each voyage with star-
perfect compass, and yearns to guide us
with fearless quiet best. Not to hear
is not a sin but what a shining
when we do, when radiance bursts from
inner stillness as our winged pilot
opening bright patterns beckoning.
If ears close, if darkness in Red Sac
gains ascent and fury fouls our flesh
with shameless feeding, our sacred guides,
still unseen, bear our unbearable,
marking, still unfelt, lifting our loss.

There Are No Quiet Afternoons

I am marked. Unknown women accost
me in streets, "I need to be punished.
Your friend said you'd whip me." Men, just met,
call me, "Master," lick my boots as I
seed their anus. Strangers seduce me
by phone, come to me in high heels and
leather, bind me, command me to kneel
for the harsh sacraments of dildo
and urine, the liquid scream of lost
words yellowed with waste and rage. I sail
these waters of pain and submission
finding ecstasy breaking with each
boundary broken. But salvation
always casts its markers deeper, like
the night-fist clenching darker inside
me. There are no quiet afternoons.

Safe Harbor

Tonight I see you run to my bed
thinking its sheets stained with murder. You
hunt the knowing arms of violence
opening your scars as you open
your thighs; balancing, awkwardly, your
blonde, suburban Surfer Girl surface
with black, urban, street-scoring rhythms,
"When we talked I listened real hard, heard
under your words and said to myself,
'He's kilt someone and it's troublin him.'
I figured you'd understand somethin.
I lost my best fren, watched her bein
beaten bad by her man 'til she pulled
her gun and run, hysterical, out
to the alley. I run after her.
See gun to her head, screamin, see her
finger tight on trigger, screamin. I
freeze. Fear squeezin my voice. Not wantin
to spark nothin I say real low, 'Stop
girl, don't do nothin crazy.' She don't
hear. Can't hear nothin but pain. Can't see
nothin but lost. Can't do nothin but
jerk her finger to God's kingdom come.

"Her scream exploded. Real time flashed and
splintered. Brain-parts splattered red bricks gray.
Eyes shut wide open. Fresh dark pool poured
its temple blessing. She had to kill
somethin. Such a pretty pearl-girl gun
do much ugly. Ignorant niggah
still in the house, 'Whydoncha bring that
damn pussy gun back in heah crazy
bitch 'fore the pohlice come!?' So I did.
Gave him a strong piece of pussy right
between the eyes like she shoulda. Cops
don't bother with no dead niggah mess.

If suicide/murder fits murder/
suicide, case closed. Sweep out the trash.

"Some nights I dream and she's there screamin.
I wake up, mouth wide open with her
pain pouring out, and I want to keep
screamin, not let go, lose her again."

She loses her wind, nestles in, her
vessel guided to a night's mooring
safer than she knows or might desire.
Our sails lower together. We drift.
I keep watch for her dream, set to sound
alarms of comfort. We can relive
the dead forever, forever lost.

Death-Winged Poetry

He marks us and mocks us. A living
death-legend, the Zodiac, urban
retiree from the killing storms, their
unmatchable pressure and release,
run out of wind to fill the hatred;
anger come to ground in soft slippers.
He glides, openly, untouchable,
wing-eyed exhibit to law's frailty;
a smirking secret on frayed side streets
of edge cities whose sprawling borders
with their beaked raptures bleed old centers,
drain their talent, darken their future,
define our century's unkempt end.

Like his victims we entered his edge
unknowingly ("If they found me they
deserved me.") visiting new friends filled
with thrilled whispers about their tall, gaunt
shuffling neighbor rumored to be the
letter-cryptic, boldly-taunting, taut
avenging angel of urban i-
solation now twenty years silent,
"They say the cops know but can't touch him."
(Looking to his yard) "When you're close, you
see his eyes Lock, heedless of light, no
Iris, just dark globes tracking dark forms."

My toddler daughter wandered away
lured by the battered red things that ruled
his back yard kingdom of litter and
dust. Alert, I approached. He appeared
towering above her. (For daughters,
good fathers are angels whose wings fold
with age.) Stooped, he tracked my formation.
His eyes thudded where once they thundered;
old hawk eyes, bold holes of lost blood lust
that hold no letters on heat gone cold.

She, squatting, heard nothing, saw only
what she touched: the faded Red Hat perched
on a red tire next to rusted gears.
With one arm he swooped her up. She looked
at him. Her eyes filled with the silent
terror of a child who sees too much.
He looked at the hat, "It don't fit no
more." The rattle in the phlegmy voice
like the whistle of a diving bomb.
An owl glided, a small snake curling
in its talons. "Bad sign." He said, "o-
men so close to the end. Troy, you know.
But Rome grew strong." "Who are you?" I asked,
"Do you not believe in God's judgment?"
"He was God's judgment." He replied, "But
he never killed no kids," (He dropped her.
I flew to her.) "that wasn't his work
call." He smiled, "But that's a dead business."
He pointed to crude hand-lettering
scrawled across his rear house wall. It read:
"OH HOW STRANGE THE STREETS OF THE CITY
OF PAIN TRULY ARE."
                    signed "—RILLKE", sic.

Owls screeched. Leaving, she gripped me tighter.
"Raptors, my love. Death-winged poetry."

The Upward Curve of Earth and Heavens

(for Megan Elizabeth)

In the morning my daughter of two
plays on my chest, the ceiling fan so
slowly wheeling above her head like
our great galaxy of history
turning above us and within us.
I want to tell her how grand we are,
how the twinkle of eternity
peeks through us, both marker and lantern.
I want to tell her we share the light
must cradle the light, nurture the light
we are. But my bright reveries stop.
My thoughts fall upon men of darkness,
lost focused men of red passions, our
deathwing superstars, who hunt and score
the worst possible game and keep us
scoring the worst with them. And I know:

I cannot protect her. From bitten
minds biting in vengeance I cannot
protect her. From exsiccated lives
with hot blood codes I cannot protect
her. From the hunger of sex for more
thrills opened and more limits broken
I cannot protect her. From feeding
beasts maned with night-trophies I cannot
protect her. From tragedy resown
as incessant nightmare I cannot
protect her. From spirits in famine
stretching dark wings I cannot protect
her. From poor luck, poor choice or poorly
conceived plans that lead to destruction
I cannot protect her. From these things
and more I cannot see or refuse
to image I cannot protect her.

And so I read to her of angels.
Show her books with paintings and drawings,
representations, of the supposed
corporeal forms of what we so
deeply desire: a corps of higher
beings commissioned to guide us Home.
And she will ask, "Da, what are angels?"
And I will tell her they are the best
(and darkest) parts of our very best
(and darkest) selves (our souls' DNA).

Deeper in her voyage when my sails
begin to furl, I will tell her how
they reached me in their dream-human form.
I will tell her how we sat and talked
over childhood's campfire smiles; how they
gave me their comfort, assured me their
protection, and deepened my trust in
the upward curve of earth and heavens.

I see our last campfire crackling—large
sparks skipping their flame to stars. I hear
crickets ringing, defining deep night.
My Friends say they are leaving (my sight
not my heart). They promise to return
whenever I call. I never call.
In moments of terror I forget
them. They do not take away the fear.
In moments of Fall or years in drift
I do not recall they are there (still)
watching (charting) failed passage. They do
not take away the pain. I breathe through
them (or they through me?) life, unfiltered.

Angels, except through us, do not reach
our beauty. They do not shun or crush
with disdain. Angels touch and transform.
Even uncalled (would chaos answer?)
they guard and guide me. Surely, they must.

Too much death has passed over my mast.
It must be marked. I must be marked, called
to witness our century's twilight,
our cities near dusk, our gathering
age, dim, in pre-dawn (the quality
of light the same). In swiftly moving
currents of unfamiliar waters
we have greater need to create what
we need. Listen. No one needs to teach
us darkness. Angels teach we are our
best (and brightest) possible angels.

Beneath the clear comfort of stars, their
compass unlocked by scholars of night
who transcribed our myths to skies (that Greek
warlords read sailing Rome's tide to Troy),
I ship my daughter to sleep. She floats
in my sails with contentment under
the furious ovens that splatter
or pattern their radiance along
the life-curve of heavens she will curve
beyond my sight; blessed with the silence
of guides she will or will not hear, and
these words, my wings, to brighten her flight.

Section III

Shorter Poems on Women

On Stone

On stone, her form still, she faced men and sky,
my first fresh death across my street not crossed.
In hot clear Spring sun, her eyes closed, lay Granny's
oldest friend, fuller than my frail twelve years,
still on her driveway stone.

Her voice, high breathy liquid gravel, still.
Her small, maid-hardened hand that held mine, offering,
gently, girl's cap for Baptism's waters, still.
Her moles, black stars in bloom that sweep across
tan fields, still visible.

That night, unseen, beneath faint constellations,
I walked the dark around her block, my shorts
unzipped, my penis leading, divining rod,
aroused, divining not divine or void
but Spring in heating flesh.

The sky she lost in sun,
the force I tracked in night,
I could not see were parts
that framed and formed a wonder:
her stars on stone, Spring still.

Two Bodies Shimmering

Manhattan afternoon, the movie line
not moving, stuck in lobby single file.
A radiant, tall dark ship of woman moored
in front of me to date who doesn't deserve
her. Harsh hushed words rush one way. Off he sails.
His absence leaving deeper harshness shushed
by tightening lips, her briefly blinking tears
that flush. I am compelled to offer quiet
presence as comfort. I ease closer: bow
to stern, mine/hers. Our contours barely touch.
Aware, she leans so slightly against me.
In trilling stillness we share sheltered brilliance.
Two bodies shimmering in rare hushed harmony.
Doors open. He reappears. We release.
I watch them flow from magic's closing port,
grateful to her, stunned by our shining shared.

Vyctoria

Huddled against this song
kneeling with the crystal emptiness,
Vyctoria, childless queen of a ruined childhood,
seedlessly dies,
dies with a hollow sound,
a heaving sobless sound,
the sound of blood retreating in needles
retreating while thighs in jagged motion
songlessly receive the broken fathers.

Her nights hold no deliverance from pain
but pain.
Arising to hunger in a season of famine
she descends her cross barren of grace,
descends with the wreckage of her song
the haggard song of those in dread
those who inject their fear in blood
and starve their lives to seedless ruin.

Hope for a First Wedding

From my childhood I felt we were coming
and I have waited in hope and calmness, doubt
and frenzy. Now, we are here and I am
so grateful, love you so dearly. There is
open light, open fields, a clear view
and the utter loveliness of your spirit,
of our spirits, seeking common higher ground.

Betrayal

Part I: Communiquè to Wife—February 14th

"The more you love the more you have left."
she said, in a Costa Gavras film.
Her lines' end marks my entrance: a man
loving you, faltering much more than
expected; still trusting, still trying.

Part II: Communiquè to Self—March 1st

You are alone, your core always alone.
She will leave and there is you only you
to fault: so distant; superior; liar
so focused on self, so accomplished at
stealth, at seducing and mastering loss.

Part III: Second Communiquè to Wife—March 3rd

You dive with a woman, you wreck with her,
reach shore with her, climb to understanding,
and build (perhaps) a civilization.
There are unions, worlds, galaxies destined.
In love more forms are possible than not.

Dream with You, Monday Night, March 7th

(End of a Marriage)

War, guerilla and senseless.
They are searching our house for their children, the wished-for
　　　survivors
who haven't. We are upstairs, hiding. You are half you and half
the one you succeeded. If they come in this room
they'll kill us. I can't find my Colt automatic.
There's only the sheath knife I grip and regrip.
Most return downstairs and out. Two young mothers remain.
I hope they'll leave, not try
this room. If they enter, I must kill quickly,
do the awful before they scream. I prepare:
knees tensed; blade held wrong side up; knowing
I must plunge and rise, catch the mouth
before alarm. The door opens. She's tall, slim,
black hair below shoulders,
a simple dress of elegance loosely worn.
The knife surprises sound, quiets her struggle,
surprisingly mild. Her friend has not seen
and enters the same end. We are alive.

Could I have spoken,
agreed not to kill if allowed silent passage?
I would not risk our lives on friendship's offer. The knife held
so little blood so easily cleaned.
In times of inner-wars
each has room for just one conscience.

Leilani

Leilani, Cancer with Polynesia rising,
waits the night away
offering staged intimacies for paying strangers.
Having touched the hard world of fenced men,
she moves with clear cautious eyes
through the adam-throated land of twilight sexes,
guarding her selves from street intrigues,
defending her secrets from casual thrusts.
She is her survival.
No nets pause beneath
poised to retrieve her miscalculation.

Astride the gorgeous above the gorge,
where age and disenchantment wait their work,
her balance is beauty, burnished gently,
reflecting the nice girls introduced home.
Her heart sees lesser introductions
from fleeting men less than desired.
In darkness, where image and penetration
often reverse, she gives herself as gift or barter;
knowing, "No one loves a queen . . . for long."
not even Miss Leilani, the dream-hearted princess,
maneuvering with care among the hurt and careless.

Thursday with a Night Moon in Pisces

(San Francisco, 3 a.m. at Studio West)

She waits your entrance to cue her performance.
There is no dance unless you ask, seek your fire
pulsing in her motion. Will you move with her?
Mount this scene with her? Descend the dark in her?
Here on the elevated floor delicacies
reel out of fashion. There are no unions,
no touchings of dreams, only a late night stage
where fantasies gag on intimacies betrayed.

On Knowing

(for Diana D.)

It was in the eyes (and the creases beneath): the saga
of struggles, incomplete, the pain of continuance.
It was in the bearing, upright and eager:
the triumph of spirit, beneficent with smile.
It was in the hips, warm and full: the curving signal
of moist acceptance for seed unsure of its flower.

These were first drafts on first sight,
the first flashing exchange of maps too quick
to be tentative, too fast to be threatening.
You, moving up to the gathering; I, staying out
with the night, knowing you did not know
how nakedly you walked; knowing you saw but did not see
the man who smiled saw his future smiling in you.

A Woman Recalling Her Molestation as a Child

It's something women just don't talk about.
No one easily unseals those secret moments
with the approved adult. No one lightly unearths
their silent guilt for unsought intrusions. But when revealed,
we find so many sharing the buried shame; the unfed
vengeance; the same, terrible unvented scream,
"HOW COULD YOU, HOW COULD YOU DEFILE ME SO DEEPLY!?"
Those slimeballs touching us, marking us
forever with their weakness. God! We were
so ripe, so helpless before their guile, their bigness.
And when we recall we are helpless again, again
the child, confused and defenseless; betrayed, alone
with our betrayal; haunted, always haunted
by the fear that we, not them, WE were responsible
for our misuse, for the markerless graveyard's
subterranean clutches. For so long
it seemed simpler, safer, to bury the dark in darkness
until cracks, once quickly patched, became fissures
insistent for light, and in their opening
was the light, the revelation of strength shared by shared hands.

The History of Civilization Is Found in Your Beauty

Today, finally, I told you how attractive you are.
That was an outright lie. You are not attractive.
You are beautiful like fabled love scenes
from haunting movies, the most beautiful woman I know.
But this does not mean we should live Casablanca,
or Casanegra. We should never make love.
For when we'd completed I could not bear to unweave
that trembling. I could not bear wearing your wetness
as secret, hoping your scent had not dawned
in mine even as I sought it. Instead,

I map your eyes' clear weather, measure
uncertain swells of your voice, and follow
the flow and flower of your hands as they open your meaning.
Do not hold these lines against me as I wish to hold
me so deeply against you. I know how to transmute
desire's brash energy. It is the history of civilization:
how oceans are charted, friendships carried, alliances saved,

poetry born. When next we meet I will smile in your weather,
embrace your hand, and a thousand ships will launch in peace.

Burial

Dark at sea the dismembered body
will not submit. Severed pieces bagged
in canvas still slash with her question,
brandish her floods. The craft is threatened.
Our history is not silenced.
Her fixated quest grieves and groans.
On shore I wait deliverance.

We stripped her from night, dragged her naked,
haunting, to hacking ground. Her head
held to stone and feet wheeled to stars
we chopped and grunted her whole to halves,
wrenched and butchered her moon to bones.
The grasping and rending of future
to past is turbulent travel.

Crafts of the heart are slowly buried.
My best is done, the rest is left,
uncertainly, to friends who sail
what I can no longer carry.

Because I loved her
loved her as deeply
as I've ever gone
does not mean I must
drown with her snared in
her unfixed compass.

Earthquake Season

(for Deborah)

The awful shaking in the north rocks my soul.
Four hundred miles south I feel its wind, an intruder
rattling my windows, stalking my friendships' deepest circles.
Is all broken?
There are no answers, no connections, only recordings,
electric tunnels. Tears become connections.
I keep them close. They keep me whole.

I hear reports: The lifeless pin the living;
they chainsaw a mother to reach her child;
to free her child they leave his leg—
serrated flesh for survival's throne.

My shelves are slipping. I call you, chastise you
for not divining my fissures,
not sensing my thief that rough shifter of plates.
I call you to call me to center.
I am here with you, home with you building our season
over rogue north winds and their promised shiftings.

Deep in night nestling with you,
slim and luminous in sleep,
my soul settles.
Surely in this clear quake weather
you can hear my heart shift closer to you.

Passage

(For my Goddaughter, Amaya,
on the day of her Batmitzvah)

I watch my daughter sleeping, as poem,
the way your father watched you, as dance,
breathe and glow, flow through your renewing
death each night, each night entered
after inspired resistance natural
at the threshold of the seeming end—
less dark when you still felt your flame so full.

Your father and I would sit and talk.
He, sometimes returning to the language
of dance, describing how he watched you
search your beat, study your marks
as you sifted the gifts and practiced the rhythms
of two impassioned racial choreographies.

There is a look a father gives his daughter
he gives no other. It comes unplanned,
unexpected, utterly naked with love
and protection. It startles and confirms
fatherhood's primacy. It settles and nourishes
like a late night rain that soothes the sleepless.

One afternoon over the trend and tinkle
of a restaurant lunch we had a darker talk.
How surprised he was to be a present father,
how joyous, how hard. How dearly he needed
respected work, how crucial, how hard.
How hard to have great promise. How hard the fear.
He shared his secrets. How hard he was on himself.
I held secret from him what I should have shared,
direct energy that simply offered would say,
"I love you. We are brothers.
I know your struggle with fear.
I know how hardened talent can become."

In time, how hardened his lungs became,
squeezing his breath and love
to bone and will and love.

> We die alone even in the arms of lovers
> holding with their deepest song.

When he died I wrote those lines. It is
one view, one truth from one life's
past place. In this place another view, another truth.

> He sleeps in peace lifted by his lover's arms
> guiding with her deepest song.

This is the heroic work for every heart,
the perfect compelling love
for the compellingly imperfect spirit
we all share. This is the threshold you cross today
more fully aflame. And with you
come imprints—a father's look, a mother's touch—
you may not remember but have not forgotten.
Each of us in purposeful passage marks another's way
becoming precious fuel for memory's campfires.

Engrave Your Life

(To be read by my daughter, lakeside, her first college year)

You read these scratchings where future's shapes
etched sharper in me my freshman year.
The waves charms of unspelled secrets spilled
their shards across my charts: "Neptune trine
moon—very good for your poetry.
Mars square Pluto—your first child will die."
(Not how her shared blood would flush against
my wader's will to darker bowels.)

At birth your heavens' geometry
was plotted, your planets housed, numbered
(buried with the lost need to treasure
stellar divinings). If the stars carve
first, living more fully deciphers.
Your wonder is the great decoder.
Dive deepest in your stillest waters,
your search will be your surest burin.

For My Wife, the Teacher,
Who Scales the Mountains Each Day

For you who scales the mountains each day
and each night descends to a waiting
mountain (and a mounting absence or
distracted presence) I raise this text
unbound with care from a binding heart
reworked to reverse my muted slide.

Where once I saw the bloom in each face
the skull now rises claiming its waste.
Each day your blooms, some stunted by want
or torn by gang-lore lures and wakes, turn
to the suns of your eyes that welcome
and nourish and lift (us) with their sight.

Our gifted mountaineer of blossoms,
I offer nothing comparable
to your shining guides prepared each day
as word-skill chapter and math-tool verse.
To the Bible of your lower back
my mouth lowers reciting my love.

Snake Wars

(write or die)

I am a warrior, veteran of snake wars,
crafter of dream-seasoned laws of defense:
to fight the serpent-priest of night, shift
your heart to self-mapped ground; deploy with care;
if he decamps, maintain strict watch
even as days descend decades.

Unwearied by time he dissects each mystery,
the soul sifted, decanted, appraised for appeal.
Smiling, he would gouge it from you, disgorge
it to you: a drying lump of defiled earth.

I have seen artists in their brightest mornings,
they shone like mountains in sun-honed air. Poised
for ascent their noon grew shadowed, fallow, falling
(swollen with fear) swallowed by night's scaled lord
like flesh by appetite.

As destruction buries an age
the high works compile, compete compress.
The stronger their witness, the clearer
their voice, the deeper their contours
impress their reliefs in our atlas
defining our passions' passage.

On my perimeter the first unsettlings:
a slash of tail beneath the suit leg; a stranger's
eyes slither away; a waiter sheds his jacket,
his new shirt glistens; scales in my water glass.
Returned—the gliding chameleon,
the presence among us hunting

I see Ulysses' daughter, mongoose-taut
and beautiful, approaching me. Wearing

destiny's fairest formula, she will
protect me. With her dark hair like towers,
certain with her maps of ancient battles,
her charts of heroes' intrigues. . . she,
he cannot defeat. Aligned with her, here
in her bare-walled house of stratagems,
we are invincible.

He is here.
His twilight uncoiled to test our defense.
He is taller, larger than a large
intense man. Fearless, she approaches.
He withdraws. She tracks his darkness,
separates us.
I listen. Is that rain
or his rasping tongue that grasps our secrets?

I hear her screams unhinged by terror,
shameless with fear and loss . . . the awful offerings
swallowed by silence. I map my ground,
a trapped man unwrapping its construction:
she was his construct,
my trust in her strength his Trojan horse.

I am naked in shallow light
unable to molt, knowing he comes
for his cold communion. Clutching my knife,
I thrust and stab, quicker, harder, wounding
only my breath, my will bleeding.

Calmly, unseen, entwined with his smile, he waits.

Our Best Life

There you are open, waiting, and I wait
wanting to open back to you again.
Unlit near death's broad noose and cure's rough scalpel,
I fear life-pieces lost more than death found.
Uncut, unsure, I pose as cut and cured,
and halved. I cheat our heart to harvest halved,
rehearsing death to have what I want heard.
In my best life I make what I want seen,
I see the last seed squeezed from my last breath.
I want to breathe earth's light with you, and fill
our best life where we starve our last best star
on too white sky that waits always for suns.

River Rafting with my Wife and Daughter

We are on our first river. Its current turns
and slides. I stroke and rudder as you paddle
your side, then mine and back. We find our rhythm.
We learn another currency of hands.

As we float there are lands, lives in collapse,
where the noon sun reflects a severed nature.
We've read they hack hands off to show they can.
We've seen the baby held by handless arms.
We do not see the orphaned hands fish feeding.

Enchantment's grace curves your hand guiding hers,
showing the better way to grip for strength.
The river's mirror ripples hands' reflections
before she leans against you sharing plums.

In ripping silence a woman fails her child.
Starving for rivers they raft our streets. Sinking,
the unmuffled mother with her howling handless
hands hurls her daughter from rooftop and follows,
screaming as they launch, screaming as they sail.

On rapids we bounce and work, reach smooth water.
We place our paddles up, glide with the river
into perfection's newest view: trout jumping,
a daughter holds her mother's hand and laughs.

Section IV

Longer Poems

Crystal and Ashes

To: Frances Elizabeth Baldwin Lennon
(February 6, 1908–May 4, 1978)

"There was a time when I was not
and after I was not I was. It is no
more wonderful that I may be again
than that I am having once been nothing."
—Charles Darwin

In near heat near summer two years after war
I came as Caesar and we both nearly died.
I cannot remember if you held too
tightly, or I simply refused, or we
jointly conspired. I do know it was
that large, boisterous insecure man who
saved us. Or so he'd have me believe (and this
time I do). He passed out cigars and bragged,
"I'll buy that boy his first piece,
start him off right!"

You'd wanted a girl
—badly—
dressed me in dresses
—early—
wouldn't cut my curls
(early blonde).

Seven was the mystical age when
my angels departed with promised
return, and desire awakened but not its means.
I wanted you.
(The opposite most familiar appeared
most obtainable.) But the Oedipal
was dressed in other complexity. I preferred
your clothes your jewelry and scents. It was
your heels that fit, not his, wherever
he was, the itinerant, philandering,
professor-king, my fathers, the true Gemini.

First, he was a giant whose
lap I loved when he rocked me
and wove his African stories; and after
always, as he tucked me to bed,
"Daddy, please, just one more?"
We peed together in mid-summer fields
while above you watched in gentle reproach
the antics of two frolicking boys.

Later, in the grinding space of crushed optic nerves
where esteem and fulfillment waiver and shatter, this
supremely high-strung arrogant man became the second
who soiled me with urine in drunken
uncontrol; attacked me as "sissy" for slowly beating
eggs; and cursed my future with the cloud of his darkness,
"One day you'll be just like me!"
                                    (and then you'll know.)

And after,
he would always seek a way for forgiveness, and
I would try because I knew he loved
me yet was helpless somehow to interior
ragings. At bitter war against himself
he guarded weakened borders, and those
he counted dearest bore the severest wounds.

I learned not to trust him and will relax
with no men, even those allowed
a guarded penetration. Most do not have
your purity of presence or muted
nobility, and neither do I with
my distance as silence masking insecurity.
Jill-womyn did, possessing eyes so defenseless
with the soul and its longing. You are both
saints. But you, as mother, are pristine with
sky; and she, as lover, was uncertain with earth.

You were the sheltered daughter reared by an
aging matriarchy, whose industrious
descendants of house-serving slaves were steadfast

to God, temperance and the party of Lincoln.
But these enduring ladies of manners
and maneuvers, who held you and child in first
affection, were the agents, unsuspecting,
of the will's castration. But he suspected,
the determined, territorial Democratic
man, son of the son of field-darkened slaves.
He would tolerate no perceived interference, and was
sensitive, in great voice, to the slightest
trespass. We were his and there would be no
crossed loyalties. But we were also theirs
entrenched on the same shaded block, and we
traveled between as couriers and prize.

It was curious for war
with its frequent stases and continued
comities. Charged undercurrents were rarely
surfaced; hostilities were never formally
declared in a struggle running decades under
sickness and graves—
a war of survival between willful survivors.

The sides, well-matched, fought through us tenaciously.
Both recruited with privileged confidence:

> "I wouldn't have married your mother
> if she carried those genes. Take Franklin,
> an addict; or slow-witted Jimmy;
> or Charles rotting with rum and TB.
> Your mother's white, Irish from upstate.
> Mrs. Baldwin adopted her while
> teaching in Albany where Frances
> would return to visit her mother."

> "Child, did your father tell you that?
> Your mother's no such thing. That's our
> blood in her—and you. I have her
> birth certificate put away
> whenever you want to see it."

(I never saw it, to ask would have been
to doubt her. And I never asked you. I knew
your husband favored exaggeration's
realm, especially with drink, though
this was confided in sober noon light.
But regardless of genes or strangers' surprise,
you were always Negro, sometimes colored,
never black or white.)

Where one camp preferred the soldier's assault:

      "Just look at those men
      they're all spineless, except for Scott,
      and not one of them's worth a good Goddamn!"

The other preferred the saboteur's grace:

      "The Lord knows your father's given
      Frances a devil of a time. But he's
      a troubled man full of fear
      and I won't say anything against him
      and neither should you, you hear?"

The soldier's barrage was effective. Most men,
both genetic and acquired, seemed passive
souls of limited purpose. The keen manipulative
will for survival was with the women;
and none held a stronger mind or sharper
tongue than your mother, Rhoda Elizabeth Graves Baldwin,

      "Oliver! Hush-up that foolishness!
      You don't have to worry about being
      kidnapped. When they find out
      what they have, they'll throw you back!"

She ruled.
Everyone deferred to my fair round
granny with the grave-blooming head, even daddy,
and those who shrouded tracks or winterized

breaths before a Sunday's audience.
Even Scott!
"Oh Lord! Here comes Scott!"
"I wonder what devilment he's found this time?"
"I just don't see how a grown man can
continue all that Tom-foolery."
The mention of Scott often inspired
called rebukes and answered lamentations
not because he flowered the darkest of a line
of fairly gray sheep (which he didn't. That was Franklin,
Jimmy's elder quicker-witted brother, twenty
years addicted to poppies and betrayal
then ten rose-years too tightly Reborn,
now five years dead found bound in the bleeding bed
slashed to closed-coffin by the untended thorn
of an unforgiven son.) but because he remained
unrepentant for his sinning in liquor
and sex. Few men so irrepressibly
enjoyed women and their irreverent pursuit.
He was a brown, full-lipped, full-bodied
man whose undistinguished height and ambition
mantled strength, and valor of extraordinary kind—
a warrior unscarred by streets in his prime.
When obstructions lingered or danger smiled, Scott was first called,
"Get Scott and tell him to hurry, you hear!"
He would come—on the run from his job or
the Bronx or the Bal-Mor-Ral Lounge. The Graves men
mostly tinkered and shied from concentration.
But Scott, when pressed, was a fixer, and with danger,
a master. His warm unyielding eyes
held the blur of its threat in constant focus.

Of all male cousins he was your favorite,
if more son than cousin. He was daddy's
favorite too (". . . except for Scott") and mine. For all
his irresponsibilities his heart was
abundant with kindness and courage. Everyone knew he could
have been more, most cast the flaw with him. But wasn't
part shared with matriarchs and another

who also held and haunted: the man of strong
youth and drained raptures, his father, hunted
and torn by railroad steel while desolate in ruptured
sleep across the last escape? If so, am I, like Scott,
hostage and spoil to worlds of war internalized:
father's masculine, their (and your) feminine?

I know my father feared the consequence
of feminine influence unbalanced,
and aggressively sought my masculine support.
But the saboteur's placement was most telling,
(". . .you hear?").
Yes, I heard him often
censuring you loudly for something soft
hardened to intrigues against his manhood; and watched
you sitting wordless in the slow
harbor of stoic tears, aligned in silence
with my stammering frailty. We both knew
you preferred me to him. At 39, after hope,
I was your miracle delivered from God,
not him. How could you stand him who
tolerated so little and demanded so much. I plotted
to hammer his skull if he ever attacked you, but
he never did. He only touched to kiss, looking
so grotesque with puckered expectation.

(At ten, sex was a welter of whispers and graphics
veiling bodies distorted by willful
contortions. I thought such scenes an adult conspiracy,
a joke on children universally shared. That beings
freely performed such repulsions was beyond
my conception. But of course we do, and do more
than I knew couldn't be done.)

He did not deserve you, deserve your
devotion. While he tended his garden
glaring with unkempt secrets, his was
the only seed you ever knew. After home
and Madison, in my years of emotional
riot, there were dreams of him: wizened after

blindness, after strokes, crawling up you leaking
his feces, hunching for his brown desire against
your ivory form. Was that the sum of your
sexual history and the matrix of mine?

For eight years I lived with you through Barbara
as husband, hunter of flesh; and father, the helpless
destroyer. In dreams your forms
would merge and lay with me. In love we discovered
our harmonies of difference; in weakness
we suffered our unsolved dissonance
clawing our rhythms to wounds.
I knew my father not as Cyclops but as me,
flawed and failing, fallen from Destiny. Flailing.

Unlike him, silence was my weapon of choice.
It could vanish her existence for hours
racking days; while, interned, the wyvern
savaged my linings. Its talons were my
talents, wasting, reversed for judgment.
My weakness tore at hers so there would tear
in me a doubled penance. She was my guilt.
I was her cross. She was her most radiant
when suffering, as if pain manifested
her strength. I could almost hear, unspoken
"Of course I should suffer, I am the stronger."
(And perhaps she was.)

Like Barbara you were devoted to one
devouring you while consuming himself.
In fear, trapped with her fish of fixed uncertainty,
she clung to love; in strength
you held as duty. You, the matriarchs'
clearest flower, learned moral rectitude
and societal contracts in narrow
exacting focus. There were no options
only God, and endurance
(and child).

Committed to a man whose life was mined; and one brief
walk from an exacting mother, you poured
your light in me as center and sum. I was
transfixed by your purity's expectations, your quiet
air of warm insistence. You were my truest
guide through definitions, and the positive
who selected its symbols. I was crystal
drawn from your wound, imbued with your will, accepting
fuel resonant to your spark. I lived your flame,
in time I would search for mine and ignite
the rebellions. You would become a symbol,
you had not intended, of independence
suspended, then lost in others' needs. You were
claimed by so much: two families,
teaching, church, sorority. Your composure
lasted to the eighth decade but where
was the time for you, for your renewal?
I felt you placed in me the hope of your perfection,
the mirror of your mother's daughter as chaste, dutiful Gemini son.

With your vessels investing their currency of dreams,
and your air, fixed and claiming, over
my sights, was I to be your prized border
state, your colony, best-loved, of extended
fulfillment? If my lands and skies were mapped for your
purpose, where was my vision to breathe? At twelve,
awareness flared to mild resistance. Fifteen, saw
sporadic refusal become open revolt implacable
before all reproach and entreaty in my
struggle to define my developing flame. Sixteen, marked
the denouement's beginning when your hold was loosened
and concordance begun. I had stared through the death you dared
not keep
(and I was mine).

Us (vs) you vs him vs us (vs) them (vs) you vs me (vs) them (vs them)
vs him (vs him) vs me (vs me): it was
a tangle of shifting fronts and alliances
in civil worlds of war unrecognized.

You were a mother forced to jihad. You saw
your child leaving you and the paths you knew correct. With your
red cross tacked to heart you were too good
for war, but your efforts were ceaseless. Even as
the taxi waited you gripped my wrists, offering
tears to God to guide and strengthen your college son.
I had to leave. You never left your mother's will.
Accepting his pride promised some balance
(your mother could never swallow his wife).
She died across the street from you.
From me, you died across a continent,
your brain slowly strangled by arteries in alarm.

Your eyes centered your purity's crystal,
each year I watched the ash levels rise.
I had abandoned you to the hammer
of his wars and the weight of my absence. I witnessed
your breaking and offered no hope. I was not
your doctor-in-residence-lawyer son
well-suited for rescue. Had you loved me
less I would have been your keenest disappointment
and not your first joy. He was killing you
and so was I. I would not return to forfeit
some part of me for more of you. As strength
is determined by honesty of purpose
you were the stronger, as measured by bald
determination he was survivor. His body
declined from his sight, eroded its linings, and yielded
most motion to three electric storms. He would
lie for hours singing with pain whose sound he withheld.
He relinquished what was taken but kept his skies,
and with them his life. And his life broke yours.
First was deep fever and the search for detection,
then slow convalescence to gradual decline
and you're whispering away,
          "I feel so tired."

Your ending was so unlike his who approached
his moment still warring, racked with waste; helpless

before the spillage of his darkness and torment
that clutched in waves, broke upon his body then
gripped again. Like an animal
clubbed beyond fear, he suffered without prehension.
An hour before death he released to acceptance.
His tides rolled to pools anointing his journey.
Had he drawn his treaty of unconditional forgiveness
and found our scars are ours for the living?

He flashed a continent
to wake me, his person
unknown, his presence
defined. He still comes in dreams.
He brings his excrement
and I am stained. When he
leaves I am clean.
I call that a settling.
I would not see his
burial. I know I must
forgive (a father gives
no choice) but I would not
offer that symbol. I love
him. I love you more.
There is more of him in me
but more of me in you
who fashioned my heart.

(I wanted to burn him like I burned you.
I dared think that by mixing your shells I could
offer in death a closeness never shared in life.)

To reach you and my forgiveness, my twins
were lost with the night moon in Pisces. Transformed to hunted,
they have lived my theater of sorrow
and confusions before blank transparent men. They were
so like him with their stupid smiles and pertly
wagging tails. ("Daddy, please just one more.") No more.
I cannot stage myself to absolution. Our debts

Madison, Wisconsin—The War Years (1965–70)

Part 1: Snowball

Snow,
balled in the dark flesh of earth,
gatherer of dust, washer of wombs,
rooted in the world's reptilian shell;
seedsman,
grizzled with beard, wrapped in your weathered, seed-torn coats,
you endure the fragments of blood-ashed lives
whose flames once dreamed in the lake-shored city.

Witness,
depositioned with myth,
the creature-secret sperm secretes through you
nourishing the seeker, anointed in silence,
fetal in the poem of the ice-carved city,
the glacial-scarred city, disfigured with beauty,
renascent with the wounds of strong, maternal fruit.

Poet,
living as poem, soiled as men and poetry
soiled with their survival,
you are not the smooth bird creature
startling the world with its god-seeking leap,
you are not the fire creature ejaculating flame
suffering in flame gravity's retreat.
You are the aging dancer of flawed choreographies
whose patient motions conserve the blood,
you are the secret possessor of weeping manuscripts
whose youth lies snarled in the burn of an age.

Survivor,
mute in dream-stained trousers,
you gather forms for an age falling formless
with flaccid flesh and famined bone,
falling with the charred testimony of burn-weary lives

skewered on fear, turning, choking, watching
the frontier flames smoke on the heavy fat, the brittle,
chordless chips; falling
formless
dream-lost
mute . . .

to the mutable constant city
uterine city flowered with youth
eager city of tempestuous moods
moon-riot city
race-charged city
city of fire and fireflight
frozen city of pelting weathers
quixotic city washed by thunder
intimate city dark with primordial silence and orgiastic scream
artisan city scrawled with polemics
learnèd city of rising mausoleums
lost city laked with asylum
drugged city of forced sleep
city of subterranean galaxies
low sensual city
venal under city
lurid city luring naked herds and lurking beasts
pedant sperm-toy city
flesh-eyed hunt city
fear-coiled serpent city
hooded city of erotic venom
constricting city of poisonous wombs
city flagrant in death's apparel
appalled with death
poem city excessive with metaphor
city maternal never was ever is
eternal with snow balled in the blood plunge.

Part 2: spring night with rose and violets

night,
my friends
comes fierce with rose
comes wild with the eye of thorns.
night,
hushed with death,
vessels the crush of our dyings.

in this closet-place of souls
where violets succumb to violence
where dance is reduced to motion,
broken rhythms and broken beginnings
punch about the air on daggered wings.
bodies collide.
mischarted collisions feed
each wound to fears.
scars return unrecognized.

on this star-starved shore
where spring reasserts its rooted knives
and skeletons of steel reapportion the night,
affections withdraw to perfumed battlements.
scaffoldings rise.
images shatter on the shivering surface
that earth-framed darkness, broad and numinous,
brooding with the soul of an ocean.

travelers,
waylaid by whispers resurrected
as screams, the rollerboard priest wheels out
his answer. his chapel skitters through guttered
sleep rattling questions shrouded since youth.
pilgrims,
uncentered in passion your air drifts
unhinged. anxious yet will-less, it hovers
near panic, the charnel-house of dreams.

voyagers in questions masked
as dreams, this night unmasks
the hunger of your question.

* * *

mai,
tracked with snow, struggles
for the pulse of another season.
knotting limbs, once expressive
with blooms, open to the
stage of the great god death.

woman,
enticing death to taste the night master,
death does not come as the postured jester
or some costumed pleaser pristine with night.
it strides in flesh as the panting spear, the
hooded presence coiled for embrace.

my lady,
from your mirror speak of the vital
mothers and the venal chartings
of contracted lovers.

> "'we gathered in ruined cathedrals
> while bombs still fell, listening to the
> silence he shared and yet never heard.
> giddily we sat with death, surprised
> that we could have the hour, move with its
> weight so well. we met death in the eye
> and the eye wavered, the knife fell out.'

"she spoke out of calmed flesh
her creature still plumed, still loving
the deafened misanthrope
who rose impassioned beyond his silence.

"now killer dreams stalk the air
my poet fills the pose of death,
he speaks and laughs and seems without commitment.
ragged hands clutch for words
weary perishable words wearing
contracts masked as pleasures.
me-for-you,
me, in your brutish air, kneeling for the liquid thorns.
me-for-you -
now, you-for-me,
you, who wears my warmth, who gathers my sleep,
who bites my cathedral while it screams."

* * *

warrior,
flailing about the world in tight formation,
you are my friend but no poet, no dancer
of words as emotional mirrors.
imperial, imperiled by your pride
asserted as defense,
your heart unsheathes its base desires.

companion,
having choked on the creature's immensity,
having lost the kingdom of folly and moonlight,
in this spring each fear anchors its seed
each seed is shaped as noose;
in you
rainbows labor out of view.

dreamer,
from your need
from its haunted motion, speak
of rapacious fathers
and the coital weave of sacrificial lovers.

"'if you live and struggle long enough
the effort will break your heart,'

"he said,
his eyes filled with a sad triumph.
he plundered each day for its possibilities
and watched each night raise their mausoleum.

"I WILL NOT WRECK
even now the island waits.
I will not always wear his ruin, know
the barricades of bodies bartering
famine for thirst.

"because she asks
no forgiveness is needed.
because her silence offers its weakness,
the night tempter circles through me
rises through me without guilt
without solace, claiming its dominion.

"yet the question remains . . .
when I enter her and she
surrounds me,
when the pain is darkened
and the spirit emptied, whose
is the possession?"

* * *

tilting with earth in a world of air
these stark words are runes lifted from fear,
amulets hoisted against the sleep of pills
and hot bath with razor.
no, my sister
you have no sleep no sultry retreat
from time's gaunt engraver
etching its diamond on soul and flesh.

walk.
late lights incline to stars.
remember the gardenia voice who
followed her day to implacable night.

she covered her creature with powdered poppies
as yours is cloaked by masked intrigue, a man
at edge who lingers near Sterling where
guileless abstractions explore decimation.

for you he waits in sky, dream-fallen,
an aging starcraft stalked by its wreckage.
sowing death, death now becomes
him: reaper, night-stalker shaken with night.
his arms uncoil to ensnare your body
now small and yellow or lean and brown.
the hands, in frenzy, pillage the throat,
shackle its breath. terror harvests the eye.
his spear, in root, ruptures your season;
the anaconda mining the bowels of a nation.

* * *

mirrored spheres lattice the lake.
a figure climbs through metal seedlings
dragging as rope his soil and seed and rose romance.
his hunger, unanswered, he answers
the dark with the knot of his question.
stars flicker and cancel.
night, the rosarian, dismantles the heartweave.

victims,
shrouded with blooms,
currents eddy throughout your air
claiming your silence, bearing
benedictions of younger dreams.

night,
my friends,
and the violence that crossed
your names ascends
as the violets of another spring.

(Note: Sterling Hall housed the Army Math Research Center
on the University of Wisconsin campus.)

Songs and Dreams on the Deaths of Fathers

(for Carol)

Part 1: Songs

Waiting the godot-carol.
Waiting with the seasons' waste
of transient tunes and idle dreams.
Waiting with the angular totentanz
in a shadow-mare of cannibalisms
and cannibalistic sexualities.
Striving to survive the fathers' dissipations.
Waiting the carol's further voicing.

Defilers of myths
pursuing the rising beast of a lower consciousness,
wild wingless men
perverting death to preserve public order,
faithless men of gifts misused
positions misapplied,
men as barbarians of sharpened mind
and highly functional intent,
whose integrities feed their professional lives.

Sons praised as heroes return as victims
turned to the rattle of their voice.
Seeing, unseen, the fathers beast-fallen,
dream-colts unfold as foals of the night mare,
unhinge with their eyes stumbling in panic
their myths, vagrant deserts, silent for rains,
torrential rains that hang in our shadows,
the purgating judgment waiting release.

Part 2: Dreams

The rains in deluge pounding
re-erecting floods in a monstrous air,
a life-soaked air, monstrously heaving.
My once stallion-keeper, in mountain forests fear-confined.
My stallion, wild with rain, pouring his soul
through towering lakes to primordial rivers
releasing history's brawling judgments.
My father, kneeling, crippled in the sobbing weather.

Voice in songs,
dark moons inlaid with dream
wet with dance in the darkened grass.
Our father, smooth and broad, pulsing with flight
seeding his youth to dream and jewel.
We, in passion beneath his flight,
in passion before his fall,
dreaming in his jeweled seed
prepared to lift his myth's downfall.

Moving within the guardian weather,
surviving dachau's cannibal-tattoo,
surviving our atoms' predatory feasts,
the rain-voice unfolds in carol,
reanointing patterns heaped in silence.
Stallions, nostrils flared, mount the rain-edge
lifting the fathers through our deaths, the renewing deaths,
who dance attendance on our dreaming procession.

Alone at the Plaza

(for Jill)

When in New York I stay alone at the Plaza.
This time was no different and neither
was the loneliness gaping like a drain
before the weakened spider. By day I conducted
my affairs and fled the night to my room
and its service. I do not venture in the city
after dark. A man should know his weakness
for others surely will. Mine is the company of women
including my wife, dead our first year, vanished;
contracts cremated, assumptions interred.
I am still young but prefer, have always preferred,
separation. I had simply surrendered to the expected
under acceptable conditions. She was gentle, more
companion, if still woman, still susceptible
to the succubus who would traduce my dreams, flatten
my sleep and fasten my waking to a surface without depth.

In my room I am safe and solitary
with a full web of personal dimension.
My reading is considerable, diverse and wise:
Rilke's angels; Dante's dark travels regard Hopkins manly
reveries; Wilson's august mystics revel
in mist over Didion's freeways, wingless, near Paradise.
Music gives me its select accompaniment:
certain towering Gregorian spinnings framing
Ravel's gorgeous layerings, Ludwig's mountainous chords piercing
Mozart's gossamer weavings. And nothing else. Nothing
except Handel's blessèd "Messiah." Each morning a passage
glistens announcing the day, affirming redemption possible
in shadows, in shadows possible angels glimmering.

Wherever I stay I photograph interiors.
I am quite sensitive to rooms. Each has its breath,
its innate source of energy. It might be

a door, or a door jamb, or the seeming
emptiness between bed and bed stand. Even
a dead room will have its grave, a marker of lament.
I have a certain patience for observation, a center
or its ruin cannot escape detection. There is
something in the texture of air, the ways shadows
bend; differences subtle but distinct to the keen
eye waiting; the camera always with me, selecting,
defining, validating my passing. I am concerned
not with technique but rather the energy of things.
I must work quickly, such energies rarely pause for fine
composition or critical focus. At best I might
capture a pulse near motion or images
nearing prefiguration; that is until room 837.

It was immediately disappointing. My window
received not Central Park, as requested, but others'
windows in an open tunnel of mechanistic grindings.
Wolfgang and I could survive a night, sketch
the core and change come morning. But night offered only
comfortless sleep, no source or its clues, no tomb
or its rubble. Perplexed, I stayed. Each day fled,
obscurely; each night entered, chartless, deepening
a space immense with mystery. Was this
a room of great lamentation, or a heaven, unborn,
preparing its shining? Shaken, I held my net
dimly in corners, waiting without counting, wanting.
Sudden, in a late Rilke night of disdainful
angels (my camera close but set
aside), lights flickered and surged.
Beneath the chandelier a figure grossly luminous, transfixing, gone.

Like a gang of wolves fear snarled at my heart, challenged my
        essence.
Darkly she returned in a shock of mirror,
her stance a shouting presence.

Terror gathered silence with wonder watching her stark grace
reach full extension within the mirror's gated face.
She passed from one to another as angels

traverse dimensions. Was her force
drawn only from glass, destined to abide
solely in reflections as revelations?

Was mine?
Was I voyeur now voyaging in her will
captive to her kingdom yet ever separate, my soul ever still?

Her movements swung to bolder definition
her axis poised on firm decision
prepared, it seemed, to shatter from illusion.

There was a hand! It lived
as one in separate worlds.
Then an arm as one in two.

Behold! Her body as message delivers its passage, triumphant.
She emerged, fetal-curled, handsome fingers clutching
glorious toes; her body stunned to rest, softly radiant.

Accepting awareness, she extended her arms across new space.
Her eyes
unfixed, revealed great sorrow, offered rapt counsel.
In a moment, a twinkling
she started to rise.
God! She was so taut
so vital and pulsing.

Her body sang with rapture and motion
as time was swallowed in energy
exultant. Her eyes, ever-dark, never regarded me
but held their vision always above. And in them
was I lifted, fixed in unison with her passion
as promise to banish isolation in victory

incorruptible. For what could unravel so exalted
a spinning by this Joan with wings transcending immolation?
Her arms passed inward over her heart, a gesture
near enchantment, preparing departure.

She stretched them outward summoning flight
and vanished to her heaven of the chandelier.

I have captured these wonders in my heart
as lens, and am bound by them with them
to her and her mystery. That I have done so
is my joy and redemption. In her sweep
of glory and darkness shines my communion
in this world and hers. She is my intercession.

I come to New York with greater frequency.
There are always affairs to be tended. I take the same room
the one with no view only back windows looking on themselves
over stone and the grind of manufactured wind. At night
she appears, my comfort, distant like dark
glass, but there, always there, only for me,
ever.

Interview with Another's Heart

> (For Laura, my dear friend on the
> tenth anniversary of her death)

If you were to state lyrically where you
are found, what would you say?

"Me? I'm not the poet, you are, remember?"

And so are you when you want to be. You only
have to give that same discipline
to words that you give to charts and numbers.

"But I'm more comfortable with numbers. Simply
by existing they're simultaneously
real and symbolic. Words aren't automatically
anything, except there. To make them meaningful,
to raise them above surface and deceit, requires
great care and patience. I'm more rewarded placing
my energy elsewhere. You're the Gemini with two positions
trine Neptune, you give yourself through words.
I'm the Pisces, the keeper of secrets,
words can't be trusted.
Do you know what I'm saying?"

Yes, but you spend so much time exploring
books, isn't that contradictory?

"No, it's really not. A good writer is a joy
and challenge. He can even be a poor
technician if his ideas are strong. Reading is simply
searching another's energy. Energy is both
form and source. Our source is the same, our form
is our signature. Mine is found on bar graphs,
horoscopes and harpsichord keys.
Do you know what I mean?"

Yes, though you must realize
how poetic you're sounding?

"Oh?
Can you tell me something? Why do I feel
like I'm being set up?"

I don't know. Do you remember the question?

"Yes, I remember.
All right, I'll try but no laughter, OK? . . .

"I am close to darkness,
to sex as communion. In them are my healing
and renewal, my release from anguish, the anxious
dinner guest chewing my desires, my unbalanced
seas, submerged, flashing unannounced. I have
my contradictions, my sight by cigarette flame.
They are my sand, my source of pearls tightly
held awaiting my fisher, my diver, unthreatened
by markerless approaches to deep water. There is
little allowance for long-term compromise, but this
is my choice, my pain of independence . . .
          How was that?"

Beautiful.

"Did you understand?"

I think so, but I've known you for ten years. One certainly
wouldn't grasp that on first introductions. I know I didn't.

"Of course not. They might see the sweet Chinese
girl, that's a popular one."

But you're not Chinese.

"I know, but you know what I'm saying.
They'll see the nice Asian girl, the one who wants to iron

and have babies; be a man's comfort;
fix him nice hot dinners; and take good care
of his cock, so good that he won't want anyone else
and if he does he'll be too worn out to operate.
Do you know what I mean?"

Is that you,
the nice girl waiting by the fire?

"Well, no, not exactly, but it's a part of me.
I'm a nice girl, really."

Oh?

"Why are you laughing?
Don't laugh, I am. You know even nice girls
can love giving great head?"

Who said anything about . . .

"I know how your mind works."

So you think you give great head?

"Are you kidding? Men, even men with just
a little imagination, look at these lips
and eat their hearts out. I watch them and pretend
I have no idea what they're thinking. It's really funny.
Do you know what I'm saying?"

Yes, but you call that the Eden look of innocence?

"This one? No, I guess I've already taken
my first bite.
                    (laughter)
                              No pun intended."

None taken, though it looks as if more than
one bite has been taken, and been enjoyed.

"Yeah, is expected to be enjoyed, and that
can lead to problems."

Because?

"Because, if his first image was the selfless sweetie
wanting only her man, and later an experienced creature
surfaced with obvious standards, that could be
a little threatening, like, 'Oh wow, there're some real
expectations here'. And there are, and much more
than sexual. And a lot of times they go unfilled.
Do you know what I'm saying? . . .You know, I don't have
the best of luck with men. I'd like to say a lot of them
were assholes but that's not fair, it's just they weren't suited
for relationships where fairness and shared
and separate space were respected. They could understand
their needs for privacy and independence but not mine.
Sometimes they couldn't even accept I had such needs.
It was just too intimidating, like, 'Oh-oh, there goes
my control'. And that was another problem because
I find it insulting when someone tries to control me.
Do you understand? But I can't blame all my crap
on men or poor luck. I have my weakness, my responsibility.
Disappointment is safer when expected,
it's the unexpected that's a bitch. Somewhere I usually
know when I'm setting up failure for protection,
and maybe that's OK. I mean, I don't know
if I'm ready to wake up to the same face
for the rest of my life. That's a little frightening
to comprehend. Do you know what I mean?
Especially if you're not familiar
with your own faces, and I'm not certain I know
all of mine . . .

"Sometimes I feel I am not myself
or at least not accepted as me. It can be real
confusing, because either someone is there
whom I don't know that others see, or others
see someone with absolutely no connection

to me, existing only in their eyes.
Do you know what I'm saying?"

What about faces you do know, like the strong lady,
the one who puts people off because she seems
so sure of herself, of her ability to get along by herself?

"I know that lady, she's a necessity.
You have to protect yourself because no one else .
will without serious strings attached. Do you know
what I'm saying? Your aura has to be strong
it must accept your responsibility. If your head
aches that's your ache and not somebody else's fuck-up."

Even if it was his hammer against your skull?

"There's the physical act and its spiritual
accountability. Out of millions
he chose me or I chose him, why? I'm not saying
the motherfucka's off the hook, I'm saying the hook
holds more than one. In this world we are responsible
for whatever happens."

For whatever?

"Yes."

Humm . . . , how far does that go?

"I know where you're going so don't, because you won't like
my answer. Barring birth defects, I don't accept
our weaknesses or circumstances as anything
other than self-decision. And really, I'm not sure
about womb-choices."

But what about Auschwitz?

"Look, you can't trample all blame under swastikas
or lock it in stars or spit it
on some rich white face, that's too easy."

But what about the decision to kill
and the killing on such enormous scale?

"What about it? I'm not trying to absolve butchers
or their masters, there's no way."

But still you think millions of people set themselves up,
were partial instruments of their own murder?
"Yes, set themselves up or allowed themselves to be. When
        someone
watches while he or others are marked and cornered
then herded towards cloaked ovens, that's a decision.
But, and I hope you're hearing me, I'm not saying
human slaughter isn't tragic or horrific
or whatever sounds you can force to speak the unspeakable.
Do you understand?"

You don't think people can love life so dearly that given
the choice of immediate death or restricted living
they'll submit to survive uncertainly?

"No, I think people can fear death so greatly
they'll surrender all dignity not to die."

Do you expect everyone when threatened
to act as saints?

"Well, saints are human,
so we have the potential."

Yes, and a lot of them are immolated, is that their choice?

"Yes, probably."

Let me see if I understand this, are you
saying that tens of thousands in Dresden and Hiroshima
decided on death and disfigurement by fire and wind?

"Look, maybe we don't always determine how or when death
        smiles,

but we can always choose how life is approached.
I'm not waiting peacefully for someone's cattle car
and my body's not soliciting anyone's bomb either.
If it happens, it happens, but only my shell will burn.
I'm half Japanese, they came for us in World War II. We were easy.
Next time they'll come for someone brown or someone black,
someone different labeled dangerous out of fear
or convenience. And I'll fight that too.
Do you understand?"

Even if it's their choice?

"In wars for the spirit we all have choices,
none are isolated. I'm not a saint and I'm not trying to be,
and I'm not demanding someone else to be.
Very few are whole enough to sing defiance
while cradling their executioner.

"But everyone has the heroic capacity
to reject blind complicity. The choice of dignity
cuts like a scream through the hangman's embrace.
And you must be careful, you don't always know whose rope is
         knotted.
Do you know what I'm saying? I know some people think
I project a certain superiority
and maybe I do. I have no apologies to make.
I wait inside my own door on my own terms.
You take me or you leave me, but you take ME
and not your conception of what I should be.
You know?"

You've gotten worked up.

"Yeah, I have. This kind of shit is serious,
it frightens me."

Well at least you haven't lost your temper. I remember
the last time you did.

"Oh...?"

Yes, let me quote you,...
       'Who the fuck is he to give me shit?
       He's just a fucking idiot!
       I don't NEED to take his crap
       I WON'T take his crap!
       Fuck him!'

"Yeah, I really lost it.
He was such a jerk, I had to quit.
That whole week was the shits. I lost it
with those motherfuckas in LA too. It's so infuriating
when people act as if you're as dumb as they are.
Do you know what I'm saying? Here's a bunch of assholes
running around LA trying to score some coke
I don't even want. You could hear their small minds
clicking, 'Well, we'll get this pretty little lady
nice and coked, and business will be a snap.'

"It was insulting. I was supposed to run around
for them for free, and believe I was being done
a favor. Finally, I just let loose. When I finished
there was this nervous throat clearing. It was really
kind of funny, they were in total shock. Here this nice,
demure Asian sweetie had just kneed them in the balls.
Do you know what I mean? I left not only with advertising
money, and they never give advertising money,
but also a job offer which I politely declined."

Politely?

"Yes. I simply told them if they wanted me to relocate
it would cost them $100,000 a year
plus an expense account. They looked so hopeless,
they couldn't tell if I was serious or not."

Were you?

"Hell yes, I was serious! My time is precious
especially when I have to spend it with idiots."

You must have made quite an impression?

"Yeah, I did. My anger hurts. I really get indignant
because I know who I am and if someone else did
that someone wouldn't fuck with me.
I guess they figured that part out.

"You know, I'm not always in control.
Often there is pain, fear that approaches
overwhelming. Some people think me less
vulnerable than I am. But I am not
on display for them, I don't pass around tears
like samples. I walk a ledge narrower than most.
It takes will to survive. I survive, so far.

"Let me tell you a dream.
There was a battle between the signpost
and the realm of the sharp theater. A man
was a killer, a stalker in cunning disguises,
who specialized in forms of hermaphrodites.
He lured you with his softness and then sprung
his trap. He sang loudly as he killed, rejoicing
in the rip and tear of flesh. His song was your
death-fear, actualized. I had seen him
in half disguise lingering over his victim.
He saw me and came snarling, hounding me through
chambers. I pointed him out and he was grabbed.
'You do not know who you have! You must be careful.
The person you have is him! I know
because I have seen him exposed.' They have to break
him down. Repeatedly they entered him and bathed him
like a woman, but still he hides. The man, the chief
breaker, bathed him and still did not know.
For my own safety, they have to realize. I scream
at him, to wake, or make him aware. 'You do not know
who you have, do you!?' But he only became angry.

I thought I could match his martial powers,
but his taunting demonstration showed me sadly mistaken...

"He was large, older and black.
I watched him deciding how to deal with me
and was afraid. I sought an alliance, 'Few men
make it to the top,' I said. 'Many try, alliances
are formed, and some get farther than if they were alone.'
'But two could make it all the way,' he said.
'Yes,' I replied, 'two could. I know him.

'I know who he is. I have certain knowledge.
You have the force, the physical strength
that is why you are the capturer of hunters,
the breaker of men. But you must be careful,
your strength is your weakness when you trust it completely.

'It makes you feel impregnable, especially
when you suspect that what you have is not your prey.
That is why this man is so insidious, those he cannot
overwhelm or for whom it is too dangerous to try
he rides their weakness like a knife, a knot, into their body.
This I know, you have the strength for the knowledge.
He is our killer, our mountain, you must be careful . . .'

"The offer waits, unanswered."

Humm, do you know what it means?

"Well, in part it means I was scared to death.
But I don't know really. It was so full of terror,
a world whose life-blood was fear. Actually, it felt
like some of your poetry, you know? I know
it was hell to escape. Once I woke up into it,
and that's a bitch when you think you're awake
and it's really a dream-part.
As a child it was different, sometimes I thought
I was a chipmunk in hibernation dreaming my life.
I guess that sounds weird, but it would have been weirder

if I'd woken up, you know? But then who knows, maybe
one day I'll wake up underground next to my nuts and berries
and say, 'Wow! Those humans are strange dangerous creatures.
It seemed so real, I thought I was trapped with them.'
But I guess that's not going to happen, and I AM
trapped with these creatures of danger. But that's my choice,
right? Maybe one only survives through fear, or maybe
fear and life's desire share the same energy.
Maybe that's all there is,
only fear, just desire,
you know?
I don't know . . .
              Why are you watching so intently?"

Because I love you.

"I know."

Section V

Closing Poems

The Maid
(For Paul Celan, suicide by drowning, 1970)

The maid again is necking by the stream.
She's done the Jew now tongues the black in shade.

She's bent for army men the Turks would bend.
She's flowed from tent to tent to lure loose blades.

Faithless she serves, faithful she cleans anew,
The maid curves down remade unmaking men.

Her skirts seined river's edge to net light's chance.
She kissed the toad, S. Fugelman's drowned lance.

She's quick for night's rash slides or slow freight's glides.
She strokes blank sticks now-stacking not how-stacked.

Voyeurs in wordless voyage are her treasures.
She never was fed pleasures passed unread.

Swallowing claimed sums, humming genocide,
the maid comes up renamed unnaming men.

The Dead They Start Their Line

The dead they start their line for me
The dead they hold a home for me
They know the shame that will not go
They know the guilt I hide with pose
They know the loss that still must grow
They know the fear I keep near soul
They know they know they know
They know the grief I should have known
They know the void I made from rose
They know the pain that I have sown
And still they make a place for me
How long the line how long the wait
The dead they hide their count from me
They count by one they count by fate
The dead they start their count for me
I know I know I know